Original title:
Echoes of the Horizon

Copyright © 2024 Creative Arts Management OÜ
All rights reserved.

Author: Simon Fairchild
ISBN HARDBACK: 978-9916-90-618-7
ISBN PAPERBACK: 978-9916-90-619-4

Shadows at the Water's Edge

Shadows dance upon the shore,
Rippling whispers, soft and low.
Footsteps fade as daylight wanes,
Secrets linger, ebb and flow.

Willows weep into the tide,
Reflecting dreams of old and new.
The twilight beckons, beckons wide,
A world where night becomes our view.

Songs Beneath the Twilight Sky

Crickets sing their evening tune,
Stars awaken one by one.
The crescent moon smiles down so bright,
A lullaby as day is done.

In whispered winds, a tale unfolds,
Of lovers lost and found again.
The twilight sky, a canvas bold,
Paints memories in golden grain.

Reverberations of Distant Light

Across the void, a shimmer glows,
Echoes of the past reside.
Galaxies in silent prose,
Telling stories through the tide.

Waves of time, they pulse and sway,
Their resonance, a cosmic song.
In the dark, they find their way,
Binding worlds where dreams belong.

Chasing the Fading Sun

With every step, the light retreats,
The horizon melts in gold.
Chasing shadows on the streets,
A tale of warmth, forever told.

Fleeting moments, time does weave,
As daylight dances into night.
We grasp at dreams we can't believe,
In twilight's grasp, we find our light.

Visions of the Shifting Sands

Whispers of the desert breeze,
Dance upon the golden dunes.
Footprints fade as night time seas,
Cradle dreams beneath the moon.

Mirages shimmer in the heat,
Pulsing like a distant beat.
Secrets held by ancient stone,
Echo tales by winds alone.

Stars twinkle in the velvet sky,
Guiding wanderers, low and high.
Each grain tells a story grand,
Written softly in the sand.

Secrets of the Celestial Veil

Beneath the cloak of night's embrace,
Mysteries twinkle, stars interlace.
Galaxies spin in timeless dance,
Inviting minds to dream and trance.

Nebulas swirl in colors bright,
Whispers flow through cosmic light.
Ancient truths in silence dwell,
Guarded well by the celestial shell.

Time cascades like a river's flow,
Revealing wonders we yearn to know.
Secrets held in celestial lore,
Draw us closer to evermore.

Candles in the Twilight

Flickering flames in dusky air,
Glimmers dance without a care.
Shadows stretch on walls so bare,
Whispers float, a soft love prayer.

Beneath the twilight's gentle gaze,
Hearts ignite in hopeful blaze.
Moments linger, sweet and rare,
Illuminated by the glare.

Candlelight holds stories old,
Of dreams and desires yet untold.
In their glow, a warmth enfolds,
As twilight's charm begins to mold.

Songs from the Silent Shore

Waves crash softly on the sand,
Whispers carried by the strand.
Moonlit tides compose a tune,
Nature's symphony, night's maroon.

Seashells hum of journeys past,
Echoes linger, love unsurpassed.
Footprints tell of those who roam,
Finding solace, making home.

Each breeze carries a secret's call,
Tales of joy and sorrow's thrall.
From the depths where shadows soar,
Emerge the songs from the silent shore.

Dreams Across the Water

Across the lake, the moonlight glows,
Whispers of dreams in twilight's prose.
Ripples dance in the cool night air,
Hopes take flight, a tranquil affair.

In the silence, secrets blend,
Shadows of wishes that softly attend.
Each reflection a tale untold,
Yearning hearts, so brave and bold.

Whispers Beneath the Stars

Under the blanket of starry skies,
Silent wishes on soft night sighs.
Constellations weave stories bright,
Guiding souls with their gentle light.

Each twinkle holds a fleeting dream,
Carried along on a celestial stream.
Voices of warmth in the night air,
Whispers of love that float everywhere.

The Language of the Sky

Clouds drift by in shapes so rare,
Painting feelings in open air.
Colors clash in a vivid dance,
Nature's canvas, a bold romance.

A gentle breeze speaks soft and low,
Secrets of winds that come and go.
The sun winks bright, a golden ray,
Telling stories of the day.

Hues of an Unfolding Horizon

Morning breaks with a brush of gold,
Promises whispered, a tale retold.
Hues of amber, pink, and blue,
Unraveling dreams that feel so true.

As daylight stretches, shadows fade,
The world awakens, fears betrayed.
In every hue, a new path lies,
An unfolding story beneath vast skies.

Murmurs in the Twilight Breeze

Whispers weave through gentle air,
Soft secrets held without a care.
As shadows dance on fading light,
The world transforms in soft twilight.

Leaves shake lightly in the hush,
While stars above begin to blush.
Each sigh of night, a tender thread,
In twilight's arms, we softly tread.

Silhouettes of Forgotten Dreams

In corners where old wishes lie,
Ghostly figures start to sigh.
Softly calling from the deep,
Echoes of desires we keep.

Through fading frames of memory,
They linger on, they yearn to be.
Each shadow dances, fades away,
In dawn's light, they cannot stay.

Phantoms of the Setting Sun

As the sun dips low and dim,
Veils of dusk begin to brim.
With colors bleeding, softly drown,
The phantoms rise in golden gown.

They swirl and weave through dusk's embrace,
Fleeting glimpses of a face.
In twilight's grasp, they stretch and sway,
Until the light is swept away.

Soft Cries Across the Sea

Waves whisper songs to distant shores,
With every crash, a heart implores.
Beneath the moon's soft, silver glow,
Cries of longing ebb and flow.

The ocean holds our dreams so near,
With every tide, they disappear.
Yet in the depths, hope's light will gleam,
Soft cries return, a shared dream.

Ancients Whispers Beneath the Night

In the quiet hush of night,
Whispers weave through silken air.
Stars twinkle with ancient light,
Secrets echo everywhere.

Beneath the branches, shadows play,
Tales of old in rustling leaves.
Moonlight dances on the way,
As the heart of darkness breathes.

Lost in dreams of those long gone,
Memories linger, soft and warm.
The night carries a timeless song,
In its embrace, I find my form.

Echoing calls of ages past,
Guide me through this endless maze.
In the silence, wonders cast,
Ancient whispers shape my gaze.

Fables of Light and Shadow

In the realm where shadows sway,
Lights and darks begin to blend.
Fables spun in dusk's soft gray,
Every twist, a tale to mend.

Glimmers peek through cloudy veils,
Chasing dreams of sunlit rays.
Murmurs ride on gentle gales,
As night weaves through the woven days.

Creatures born of dreams unfurled,
Dance beneath the starry dome.
In this wonder, time is twirled,
And every heart can find a home.

Oh, the stories yet untold,
Hidden in the folds of night.
Fables of the brave and bold,
In the clash of light and sight.

Cradled in Celestial Absence

In the stillness of the void,
Celestial thoughts drift and sigh.
Stars may fade yet are not destroyed,
In absence, they learn to fly.

Cradled in cosmic embrace,
Time dissolves with every breath.
Softly lost without a trace,
In the dance of life and death.

Whispers brush against the dark,
Carrying dreams across the space.
In silence, they leave their mark,
Each heartbeat holds its own grace.

From the depths of nothingness,
Beauty blooms in unseen ways.
Cradled here, I find my rest,
In the stillness, hope displays.

Pathways of Resplendent Dreams

In twilight's glow, the paths unfold,
A journey traced in silver beams.
Footsteps silent, stories told,
We wander through our waking dreams.

Stars align to mark the way,
Guiding souls with gentle light.
Through the night, they hum and sway,
Creating magic in their flight.

Every step, a wish released,
Floating softly on the breeze.
In each moment, heart's a feast,
As the world bends, bends with ease.

Underneath the vast expanse,
Hope ignites in every seam.
Follow softly, take your chance,
On the pathways of resplendent dreams.

Faint Memories of the Shoreline

Waves whisper softly, secrets untold,
Footprints of laughter, warmed by the gold.
Time drifts like shadows, across the wet sand,
Gone are the moments, we let slip from hand.

Seagulls are calling, their cries fade away,
In the back of my mind, I hear them play.
Salty air dances, a memory's plume,
Echoes of joy, in twilight's soft gloom.

Lullabies of the Setting Sun

Crimson skies cradle the day's slow retreat,
Whispers of twilight, a gentle heartbeat.
Stars blink awake, the night keeps its tune,
Dreams cuddle close, beneath the soft moon.

Shadows are weaving, a tapestry bright,
Lullabies linger, in the depth of night.
Fading light kisses the earth with a sigh,
As time holds its breath, and wishes goodbye.

Stories written in the Sand

Tales of adventure, etched by the tide,
Whispers of ages, where secrets abide.
Footsteps of wanderers, lost in the flow,
Dreams wash away, like the ebb and the glow.

Shells speak in colors, of worlds never seen,
Each grain a memory, in spaces between.
Laughter and echoes, caught in the breeze,
Stories unravel, like leaves from the trees.

The Horizon's Silent Call

Endless expanse where the sky meets the sea,
A silent beckoning, just waiting for me.
Promises linger on the edge of the day,
As waves whisper softly, urging to stay.

Clouds drift like dreams across sunset's embrace,
Painting horizons with beauty and grace.
The call of the wild, in the heart beats aligned,
Guiding my spirit, to leave doubt behind.

Whispers from the Distant Shoreline

Waves crash gently on the sand,
Secrets carried hand in hand.
Shells hold stories from the deep,
Where the ocean's shadows creep.

Seagulls call in the salty air,
While the sun begins to share.
Colors bleed into the sky,
Painting dreams as time drifts by.

Footprints trace a silent song,
Echoes where the heart belongs.
Beacons shining through the night,
Whispers dance in soft moonlight.

As tides rise and the daylight fades,
Hope awakens, never swayed.
On this shore, our spirits soar,
Forever drawn to wander more.

Twilight's Soft Embrace

A gentle hush wraps around,
As daylight dims without a sound.
Softly twinkling stars appear,
In the twilight, dreams draw near.

Shadows blend with the fading light,
Whispers claim the coming night.
Golden hues begin to fade,
Painting skies in twilight's shade.

Breath of evening cool and calm,
Nature's voice, a soothing balm.
Laughter echoes in the breeze,
Wrapped lovingly among the trees.

As night unfolds its velvet cloak,
Silent tales in darkness spoke.
Embraced by stars, our wishes gleam,
In the quiet, we can dream.

Resonance of the Fading Light

In the dusk, a whisper flows,
As the light begins to close.
Golden rays, a fleeting grace,
Casting shadows, time's embrace.

Fluttering leaves in evening air,
Carry echoes everywhere.
Reflections weave through fading heat,
As day concedes to night's retreat.

Pale horizons softly gleam,
In the quiet, we can dream.
Moments linger, heartbeats blend,
In this space, where time can bend.

With every breath, the silence grows,
Whispers of the night bestows.
Holding close the day's last light,
A dance of shadows, pure delight.

Pathways to the Distant Dream

Winding paths through fields of gold,
Stories waiting to be told.
Every step a journey new,
Guided by a heart so true.

Stars above with secrets bright,
Map the way towards the light.
In the breeze, a melody,
Calling forth sweet reverie.

With each turn, the world unfolds,
Sparks of wonder to behold.
Colors splash across the scene,
In this quest, we uncover dreams.

Hand in hand, we wander far,
Chasing down the evening star.
Pathways lead where hopes take flight,
In the dawn of endless night.

Reflections Floating on the Surface

On the water's glassy sheen,
Memories dance, bright and keen.
Images of moments passed,
Whispers of the diecast.

A ripple breaks the quiet night,
Echoes of the fading light.
Thoughts like boats drift and roam,
Searching for a place called home.

Beneath the moon's soft glow,
Secrets of the deep we know.
In the calm, we find our trace,
Each reflection holds a face.

Floating dreams with each tide,
In the silence, we confide.
Rippling whispers on the shore,
Time and tides forevermore.

Seeking the Beauty Beyond Dusk

As daylight fades to shades of gray,
Night beckons in a gentle sway.
Stars begin to sparkle bright,
Guiding hearts through velvet night.

The horizon's brush, a painter's hand,
Crafts a dreamscape, vast and grand.
In every hue, a story told,
Of whispered hopes and glimmers bold.

Fading warmth, the coolness climbs,
Nature's rhythm in silent chimes.
With every breath, we yearn to see,
Beauty that's promised beyond the tree.

In dusk's embrace, we linger long,
Searching for where we belong.
Embracing shadows, we find grace,
In this twilight, a sacred space.

Hues of Longing at Eventide

Cascading colors fill the sky,
Brushstrokes where the shadows lie.
The sun dips low, its golden crown,
Painting dreams of coming down.

Every twilight whispers soft,
Lifting spirits, hearts aloft.
With each shade, a hope unfolds,
In these colors, tales retold.

A longing lingers in the air,
For things that once were truly fair.
As night begins its stealthy climb,
We chase the echoes lost in time.

Yet in the dusk, a spark ignites,
Stirring passions, heartfelt flights.
Eventide, with hues so bright,
Awakens yearnings, pure delight.

Soft Light Beneath the Starlit Canopy

In the hush of night's embrace,
Stars assemble, grace in space.
A blanket sewn with threads of dreams,
In quiet moments, silence gleams.

Soft light spills from skies above,
Dancing softly, speaks of love.
Each twinkle tells a tale anew,
Woven whispers to guide us through.

Underneath this cosmic dome,
Hearts alight, we find our home.
In the stillness, every sigh,
Is a promise as the world goes by.

Beneath this starlit canopy,
We discover who we dare to be.
In shimmering glow, we connect,
With the universe, we reflect.

Fragments in the Evening Light

The sun dips low, a golden hue,
Casting shadows on the dew.
Whispers of the day draw near,
As twilight paints the sky sincere.

Colors bleed in gentle grace,
Time slows down, a sweet embrace.
Echoes of the day's delight,
Fade softly in the evening light.

Crickets sing a soothing song,
Nature hums where we belong.
Stars awaken, shy and bright,
Guiding dreams into the night.

With each breath, the world stands still,
Moments captured, hearts to fill.
Fragments of a day gone by,
Glimmers in the fading sky.

Traces of the Wandering Stars

Across the vast and endless sea,
Stars like whispers call to me.
They twinkle tales of ancient lore,
Mapping paths to distant shores.

In the night, their dance unfolds,
Secrets shared that time beholds.
With each wink, they seem to say,
Find your way, don't drift away.

Galaxies in the velvet black,
Each a story on its track.
Tracing dreams through cosmic light,
Wandering stars ignite the night.

I close my eyes and make a wish,
To ride the waves of starlit bliss.
In the silence, sweet and deep,
The traces linger as I sleep.

Harmonies of the Distant Sky

In the cradle of the night,
Harmony takes gentle flight.
Notes of starlight softly weave,
Songs of skies that never leave.

Clouds adrift in twilight's glow,
Cradling whispers from below.
Each melody a cosmic sign,
Reaching hearts, both yours and mine.

Underneath the vast expanse,
Dreamers lost in starry trance.
They listen for the music's thread,
Harmonies that can't be shed.

In the evening's calming breeze,
Nature sings, it aims to please.
With each note, the soul finds peace,
In the sky, all worries cease.

Glimmers of the Wandering Breeze

A gentle sigh through fields of green,
The wandering breeze, a serene queen.
It carries voices, soft and light,
Dancing dreams into the night.

Through the trees it weaves and flows,
Bringing tales of where it goes.
Every whisper, every tease,
Are glimmers held in wandering breeze.

Sun-kissed petals start to sway,
Beneath the warmth of fading day.
Nature's breath, a calming ease,
A lullaby in evening's tease.

And when the stars begin to gleam,
The breeze will carry every dream.
In its song, our hearts will find,
The glimmers of the night unwind.

A Journey to the Edge of Light

In twilight's calm, shadows play,
A path unfolds, where dreams stray.
The horizon gleams with whispers bright,
We step beyond, into the light.

Stars awaken, one by one,
Guiding us 'til the night's undone.
With every step, the world ignites,
A journey begins, to chase the light.

Through valleys deep and mountains wide,
We search for hope, with hearts as guides.
Each breath a promise, each glance a spark,
We wander forth, into the dark.

Boundless skies, we lift our eyes,
To dance with dreams, where freedom lies.
In the embrace of dawn's first glow,
We find our way, let courage flow.

Whispers Beyond the Dusk

The evening sighs, soft as a breeze,
Carrying tales among the trees.
Each rustle holds a secret near,
In whispers soft, we learn to hear.

The stars begin their gentle quests,
Cradled in night, the silence rests.
With every shadow, stories weave,
In twilight's arms, we dare believe.

Floating on the scent of dew,
The world embraces, fresh and new.
As darkness falls, our dreams take flight,
Homeward bound, we chase the night.

In quiet moments, hearts align,
The echoes blend, yours with mine.
Together we roam, hand in hand,
In whispers soft, we understand.

Reflections on the Edge of Day

As dawn breaks soft, the world awakes,
Mirrors of light on the still lake.
Each ripple holds the sun's embrace,
In its warm glow, we find our place.

Golden hues dance on the shore,
While shadows whisper of tales of yore.
Every moment, a chance to see,
Reflections of hope, wild and free.

With each new light, our spirits rise,
Underneath the vast, open skies.
Embracing change, we learn to play,
Finding our path on the edge of day.

Time flows onward, like a stream,
Carrying with it, every dream.
In the quiet hour, hearts will sway,
Together we linger, just a stay.

Mists of Tomorrow's Dawn

In morning's grip, the mist unfolds,
Secrets wrapped in haze, untold.
Each step we take, through veils of gray,
With every breath, we light the way.

Whispers linger in the trees,
Carried gently by the breeze.
In the quiet, the world holds tight,
Embracing shadows, chasing light.

The future calls from beyond the fog,
A promise rests in every log.
As daylight breaks, our fears are drawn,
Into the warmth of a brand new dawn.

Misty dreams begin to clear,
Hope emerges, bright and near.
With open hearts, we greet the day,
In tomorrow's light, we find our way.

Lullabies of the Rising Moon

Whispers soft in the night air,
A melody carried from somewhere.
Crickets sing, the shadows play,
As the day's worries drift away.

Misty beams light up the dark,
Guiding dreams with a gentle spark.
Each sigh of wind a tender tune,
Wrapped in lullabies of the moon.

Stars wink sweetly in the deep,
Guarding hopes as we fall asleep.
Cradled in the night's embrace,
With dreams waiting in quiet space.

Hold your breath as wonders bloom,
In the arms of the rising moon.
Sleep tight, let your spirit soar,
In this night, forevermore.

Dreams in the Golden Afterglow

Sunset paints the sky a hue,
Whispers golden, soft and true.
Fading light, a gentle sigh,
Telling tales of days gone by.

Dreams awaken in twilight's kiss,
Moments wrapped in soothing bliss.
Hearts may wander, hopes ignite,
In this glow, all feels right.

The horizon breathes a secret song,
Where the past and future belong.
Caught between the dusk and dawn,
In this warmth, we carry on.

Golden visions dance in minds,
Echoing the paths we find.
In the stillness, let love flow,
Cradled in the afterglow.

Enigmas of the Vanishing Path

Footprints linger where grass bends,
Whispers hide, the story sends.
Through the mist, a shadow glides,
On the path where mystery hides.

Leaves murmur secrets untold,
Fables of the brave and bold.
With each step, the echo fades,
Lost in dreams, the light cascades.

Twisting trails through ancient trees,
Rustling leaves and sudden breeze.
Where will the winding journey lead?
In silence lies the heart's true need.

Chasing twilight, we explore,
Finding clues forevermore.
On this path, so strange yet clear,
Enigmas bloom, ever near.

Echoing in the Starlit Silence

In the stillness of the night,
Stars emerge, a wondrous sight.
Whispers dance in the cool air,
Secrets linger everywhere.

Moments stretch like shadows long,
Carried forth, a timeless song.
Hearts entwined, together here,
In the silence, all is clear.

Reflections shimmer on the lake,
Truths revealed in the still break.
The cosmos hums a gentle tone,
As we wander, never alone.

Each heartbeat echoes in the night,
Guiding us with softest light.
Together, in this vast expanse,
We find solace in the dance.

Memories at the Water's Surface

Beneath the sky's vast dome,
Reflections whisper soft and low.
Each ripple tells a tale of home,
Where dreams and memories flow.

Time slips by in gentle waves,
Carrying echoes, sweet and clear.
In every splash, a heartbeat saves,
A moment held forever near.

Glimmers dance on twilight's face,
As shadows stretch and drift away.
The water cradles every trace,
Of laughter shared in yesterday.

Silent oars dip in the light,
Guided by the stars above.
In silence, we embrace the night,
Bound by whispers, thoughts of love.

Tides of Time's Fading Glow

Softly flows the evening tide,
Embers fade with sun's descent.
In the breeze, our dreams abide,
Echoes of what once was spent.

Moonbeams kiss the water's skin,
Casting silver on all that's past.
In the glow, the heart can spin,
Unraveling memories so vast.

Each wave a moment, fleeting, dear,
Rising high, then sinking low.
In the calm, we hold what's near,
A treasure chest in time's slow flow.

As tomorrow's light draws near,
We cherish every fleeting hour.
In the depths, we cast our fear,
And find strength in the fading power.

Celestial Serenade at Dusk

Stars awaken in twilight's song,
A chorus woven through the night.
Each note a wish, where dreams belong,
Illuminating hearts so bright.

The moon, a lantern in the sky,
Guides our thoughts on gentle streams.
As constellations drift and fly,
We trace the paths of hidden dreams.

Whispers of the cosmos call,
Drawing soulmates from afar.
In this serenade, we feel small,
Yet infinite, like every star.

As evening blooms and shadows play,
Let the stars lead us tonight.
In their glow, we'll find our way,
In a dance of love and light.

Ripples in the Evening Calm

Stillness blankets the tranquil sea,
Where colors pulse in soft repose.
Ripples echo, wild and free,
Telling tales the water knows.

In the hush of twilight's embrace,
Each wave a sigh, a fleeting thought.
As the horizon finds its grace,
We ponder moments time has wrought.

Starlit skies above us gleam,
The dusk unfolds its velvet cloak.
In the quiet, we share a dream,
As gentle waves of silence spoke.

With every ripple, we're entwined,
In this serene and sacred place.
Together, always intertwined,
In evening's calm, we find our space.

Night's Gentle Tapestry

Stars flicker in the night,
Whispers of dreams take flight.
Moon drapes silver on the ground,
Quiet magic all around.

Soft winds carry tales so old,
Chanting secrets, brave and bold.
In the hush, the world stands still,
Night's embrace, a tender thrill.

Shadows dance beneath the trees,
Rustling leaves in gentle breeze.
Coolness wraps the earth in grace,
Night holds time in warm embrace.

Sleepy eyes begin to close,
Underneath the fragrant rose.
In this peace, the heart will sway,
Finding joy in night's ballet.

Layers of the Unseen Path

Where the shadows intertwine,
Footsteps mark the edge of time.
Paths layer deep with tales untold,
Within each twist, secrets unfold.

Life's journey flows, a winding stream,
Every turn a fleeting dream.
Beneath the surface, roots connect,
In every heart, a hidden quest.

With each step, the past remains,
Echoes linger, joy and pains.
Veils of mist conceal the way,
Yet guide us onward, day by day.

In the quiet, shadows play,
Guiding hearts that roam away.
In layers deep, we find our truth,
Journey's wisdom, timeless youth.

Twilight's Lingering Embrace

The horizon blushes red and gold,
As day surrenders, softly bold.
Twilight dances, fades to night,
Hues of magic, pure delight.

Whispers weave through dusky air,
Promises tucked in evening's care.
Stars awaken with a sigh,
As daylight bows and bids goodbye.

Moonlight bathes the world in peace,
Fragile moments never cease.
In twilight's gentle, warm embrace,
Time stands still in this soft space.

Lost in dreams that softly call,
In twilight, we can have it all.
As the night unfolds its charms,
We find solace in its arms.

Fragments of Time Beneath the Stars

A canvas spreads in endless night,
Stars like diamonds, pure and bright.
Moments frozen, softly gleam,
Fragments of a fleeting dream.

Each twinkle tells a story old,
Of love and loss, of dreams retold.
Underneath this cosmic shroud,
In silence, our hopes are loud.

Through the darkness, hearts align,
Echoes of the grand design.
Time slips by, yet here we stand,
Bound together, hand in hand.

Underneath the stars we share,
Whispers float upon the air.
In fragments, we find unity,
In this night, our tapestry.

Laments of the Wandering Tide

Whispers of water call my name,
Waves roll softly, never the same.
Each ebb and flow, a tale to unfold,
Stories of journeys, both timid and bold.

Moonlight dances on a cresting wave,
In its embrace, the sea's heart is brave.
Yet deep within, the sorrow lingers,
Ghosts of ships lost to unseen fingers.

Upon the shore, the shells sigh low,
Fragments of life in the undertow.
Dreams drift far beyond the line,
As I chase the tide, forever divine.

Secrets of the Sunlit Sea

Beneath the surface, secrets blend,
Where light meets shadow, stories bend.
Coral castles wrapped in delight,
Guardians of wonders, hidden from sight.

Golden rays chase the playful fish,
Flickering jewels, a shimmering wish.
In rippling whispers, the sea confides,
Truths of yesterday where mystery hides.

Gentle waves carry dreams softly ashore,
Echoes of voices, forevermore.
The sun sets low, igniting the blue,
As night descends, the stars are anew.

Rhythms of the Dusk Sky

As daylight dims, the colors twirl,
Crimson and violet in a radiant swirl.
Silhouettes dance on the edge of night,
The world holds its breath, basking in light.

Clouds drift slowly like whispers of time,
Each moment fleeting, a rhythm sublime.
Stars pierce the veil, eager to gleam,
In the canvas of dusk, I lose my dream.

A chorus of crickets begins to sing,
Nature's embrace, in twilight's wing.
The heavens echo with celestial grace,
In the heart of dusk, I find my place.

Footprints in the Dimming Light

Wandering paths where the shadows grow,
Each footprint whispers of journeys below.
Memories linger, soft as a sigh,
In the fading light, where old dreams lie.

With every step, I trace the past,
Echoes of laughter, moments that last.
Time paints the ground with stories to tell,
In the silence of twilight, I bid farewell.

The horizon blushes as day fades away,
With hope in my heart, I choose to stay.
For in the dimming light, there's a spark,
Guiding my journey, igniting the dark.

Chimes from the Far-off Waves

Whispers ride on ocean's breath,
Notes of salt and distant quest.
Each wave a song from deep below,
   Chiming softly, stories flow.

Stars above begin to gleam,
Casting light on water's dream.
The tide rolls in with gentle grace,
Recalling time, a rhythmic trace.

The moon reflects on shifting blue,
Dancing shadows, night anew.
Every surge a call to hear,
Melodies that pull us near.

Embraced by night, a tranquil balm,
Waves' chimes weave a soothing psalm.
From far-off shores, they drift and sway,
In harmony, they fade away.

Visions at the Brink of Night

As daylight wanes, the colors blend,
A canvas where the shadows mend.
Crickets chant their evening song,
While dreams beckon, sweet and strong.

The horizon blushes, soft and rare,
Whispers of secrets fill the air.
Stars flicker with a knowing glance,
Inviting us to join in dance.

In twilight's hush, the world decays,
While hope ignites, and fear betrays.
All that's lost begins to rise,
In twilight's heart, the spirit flies.

Visions swirl in shades of night,
Guiding hearts toward the light.
Each moment holds a hushed delight,
As dreams unfold at the brink of night.

Tales Carried by the Breeze

Softly through the branches sigh,
Whispers of the past float by.
Stories woven in each gust,
Carried forward, iron and rust.

Leaves converse in playful tones,
Echoing the heart's sweet moans.
Ancient tales of love and loss,
Nature sings, no line is crossed.

Across the fields, the secrets glide,
In each breeze, our hopes reside.
Moments captured, spirits free,
As life unfolds in mystery.

From mountain high to valley low,
Tales of old continue to flow.
In every breath, stories tease,
Embraced by whispers of the breeze.

The Last Glow of Day

Golden rays begin to fade,
Painting skies in soft cascade.
All the world turns calm and still,
As time dances, pure and will.

The sun dips low, a final bow,
Embracing dusk, it takes a vow.
With colors rich, the evening spills,
As shadows lengthen on the hills.

In the silence, night is born,
Wrapped in twilight, dreams are worn.
Each moment lingered, breath held tight,
Fleeting beauty of the night.

The stars prepare their twinkling show,
A guiding light in evening's glow.
The last whispers of the day,
Fade gently, drifting far away.

Traces of Forgotten Dreams

In the quiet corners of the mind,
Faded whispers linger and unwind.
Secrets tucked in shadows deep,
Echoes of the dreams we keep.

Fragments of laughter, light and air,
Moments lost, beyond compare.
A tapestry of hopes once bright,
Now veiled in the soft twilight.

Traces left where shadows play,
Ghosts of wishes drift away.
In the silence, they still gleam,
Threads of our forgotten dream.

Yet in the heart, they softly glow,
Reminders of what we used to know.
Though time may steal, and fate may bend,
The dreams we had will never end.

Reflections in the Gloaming

When the sky turns shades of grey,
And whispers bid the night to stay,
Reflections dance upon the lake,
Casting dreams in twilight's wake.

The stars awaken, one by one,
As day retreats, and night is spun.
Softly glows the moon's embrace,
Guiding lost souls through this space.

In the stillness, secrets sigh,
The echoes of a night gone by.
Each ripple tells a story true,
Of all the paths we wandered through.

As shadows stretch and silence reigns,
Within the heart, a longing gains.
In gloaming's light, we find our way,
Through silent dreams, till break of day.

The Pulse of Distant Sands

Beneath the stars, the desert hums,
A heartbeat soft, as night succumbs.
Golden grains like whispers flow,
Carrying tales of long ago.

Footprints traced in twilight's hue,
A journey bold, a tale anew.
Winds of change sweep through the land,
The pulse of time in distant sands.

Echoes of ages lost to sight,
In the silence, stories ignite.
Every grain a life once lived,
From sun scorched days, we now forgive.

In the vastness, dreams expand,
Connections forged on shifting land.
With each breath, the past remains,
The throbbing heart of endless plains.

Silhouettes in the Evening Mist

In twilight's cloak, the shadows dance,
Figures whisper, lost in trance.
Silhouettes against the fading light,
Stories born in the heart of night.

Misty echoes swirl and sway,
Memories from a distant day.
Fleeting glimpses of what once was,
Haunting dreams without a cause.

Through murky veils, their secrets hide,
Lifetimes lived on time's swift ride.
A breath away, yet far from reach,
Lessons whispered, life to teach.

Together they weave a tapestry,
Of lost hopes and mystery.
In the stillness, they softly kiss,
The fleeting truth in evening mist.

Sighs of the Glistening Sea

Waves whisper soft secrets,
Under the silver moon's glow.
Each tide tells a story,
Of dreams lost long ago.

Seagulls dance on the breeze,
While salt clings to the air.
A gentle lullaby plays,
As I breathe in despair.

Footprints fade on the shore,
Washed away by the night.
Memories flicker like stars,
In the vastness of light.

The sea has its own voice,
A hymn both wild and free.
In every sigh and swell,
I find a piece of me.

Reflections of a Wandering Heart

In the quiet of twilight,
I search for familiar roads.
Each path leads to the silence,
Where the restless heart explores.

Moonlight guides my footsteps,
Through shadows of the past.
Every turn reveals secrets,
That forever linger, vast.

With each pulse of the night,
Hope dances in the dark.
A bonfire of desires,
Igniting every spark.

A journey without end,
Yet I wander with grace.
In the labyrinth of dreams,
I find my sacred place.

Latticed Shadows and Distant Echoes

Through the lattice of branches,
The sun spills golden light.
Shadows play on the ground,
Transforming day into night.

In the distance, an echo,
Of laughter, soft and sweet.
A reminder of moments,
That time can't quite defeat.

Flickering lights in the dusk,
Guide the soul through its quest.
With each step that I take,
I feel the universe rest.

Tangled in whispered dreams,
I walk this path alone.
Yet in shadows and echoes,
I find my heart has grown.

Light woven through the azure veil

Above, a sky unfurls,
In hues of softest blue.
Clouds drift like gentle thoughts,
While sunlight breaks on through.

A tapestry of colors,
Weaved with a tender hand.
Each ray, a brushstroke bright,
Painting the sky so grand.

Beneath this azure canvas,
I bask in the embrace.
With every beam and whisper,
I find my sacred space.

Light dances on the water,
A glimmer in the breeze.
In this woven moment,
I find my heart at ease.

Whispers of Distant Shores

Soft sands cradle the tide,
Seagulls cry in the breeze.
Footprints fading, where waves slide,
Time whispers through the trees.

Stars twinkle in the night,
Guiding dreams on silver glow.
Moonlight dances, pure delight,
As the ocean's rhythms flow.

Shells tell tales of the deep,
Secrets buried in the sand.
Waves that crash, the lullabies keep,
Nature's treasures, softly planned.

In the distance, ships will roam,
Echoes of adventures past.
Whispers call us, lead us home,
To the shores where dreams are cast.

Reverberations at Dusk

Shadows lengthen, colors blend,
Daylight wanes, but still we stay.
Whispers linger, time can bend,
  In the twilight, hearts at play.

Gentle breezes brush the leaves,
As night unfolds its velvet shawl.
Softly sighing, the world grieves,
  In fading light, we hear the call.

Fires flicker, laughter soars,
  Crisp echoes in the gathering night.
Life's small wonders, we adore,
  In the dusks that feel so right.

Stars awaken, one by one,
  Promises of a peaceful rest.
In reverberations, the day is done,
In each heartbeat, we feel blessed.

Murmurs from the Edge

Where land meets the wild embrace,
Whispers rise, the currents play.
Nature's secrets find their space,
In the twilight's soft array.

On cliffs high, the wind confides,
Stories woven, old and new.
In silence deep, the heart abides,
A melody that stirs the blue.

Beneath the moon's watchful grace,
The ocean's pulse, a soothing balm.
In the shadows, dreams we chase,
Murmurs trailing, sweet and calm.

Each breath carries tales untold,
Of adventures beyond the waves.
In the hush, our hearts unfold,
To the whispers that nature saves.

Resonance of the Setting Sun

Golden hues paint the sky,
Day's last breath, a soft goodbye.
Clouds blush with a fervent sigh,
As night draws near, shadows lie.

On the horizon, colors blend,
A canvas vast with every hue.
Sunset's beauty, time to spend,
In its warmth, we start anew.

With every note, the world sings,
Birds in flight, the sky ablaze.
Nature's voice, as daylight clings,
In this moment, souls amaze.

As dusk embraces the land,
Hearts reflect the glow it sends.
In the silence, hand in hand,
We find solace where darkness bends.

Shadows on the Water's Edge

Shadows dance upon the waves,
Whispers of the night they crave.
Moonlight spills on liquid glass,
While the stars in silence pass.

Ripples spread where darkness sighs,
Echoes of the fading cries.
Branches stretch like fingers long,
Cradling secrets in their throng.

Nighttime brings a gentle peace,
As the world finds sweet release.
In this stillness, hearts can soar,
Searching for what lies in store.

Breezes carry tales untold,
Of forgotten dreams grown cold.
At the water's edge we stand,
Linked forever, hand in hand.

Songs Beneath the Twilight

Notes of evening rise like mist,
In the air, where dreams persist.
Gentle hums from crickets play,
As the light begins to sway.

Colors blend in soft embrace,
Daylight fades without a trace.
Chasing shadows, hearts unite,
In the songs of coming night.

Stars emerge with brilliant gleam,
Painting skies with hopes that dream.
Whispers curl like smoke in air,
Tales of love and quiet care.

In the twilight's gentle fold,
Wisdom lies, and truth is bold.
We gather strength from what's around,
In twilight's songs, our peace is found.

Calls from the Beyond

Voices echo from the past,
Calling softly, shadows cast.
Through the veil, a bridge does form,
To the lost, a promise warm.

Footsteps blink on misty shore,
Guiding us to seek for more.
In the stillness, silence speaks,
Answers found in time's mystique.

Tides of time will ebb and flow,
Filling hearts with what we know.
From the darkness, light will rise,
Brightening the starry skies.

In the distance, hear the call,
Softly rising, in a thrall.
With each heartbeat, dreams are spun,
As the night embraces dawn.

The Lure of Fading Light

As the sun dips down with grace,
Shadows lengthen, fill the space.
Colors shift from bright to gray,
In the twilight, night holds sway.

Whispers of the day take flight,
In the lure of fading light.
Every shadow casts a tale,
A soft memory, a gentle veil.

Stars peek out, their promise clear,
Guiding dreams that linger near.
In the hush, the world takes breath,
Finding peace beyond the depth.

Let the twilight draw you close,
In its arms, you'll find repose.
In the quiet, souls ignite,
Chasing echoes of the night.

Shadows of Memory on the Water

Whispers float upon the stream,
Echoes of a distant dream.
Glimmers dance with fleeting grace,
In the twilight's soft embrace.

Reflections shimmer, fade away,
Carried by the rippling sway.
Fragments of the days gone by,
Kissed by stars in evening sky.

Beneath the moon's enchanting glow,
Memories drift, they ebb and flow.
Waves of time, forever spun,
In the quiet, we are one.

Let the waters tell their tale,
Of love found and hearts that fail.
In the shadows, truth resides,
On the surface, still it hides.

A Symphony of Fading Light

As the sun begins to wane,
Colors blend, a soft refrain.
Notes of amber, crimson hue,
Play the skies, a perfect view.

Gentle breezes start to sigh,
In the dusk, we watch and lie.
Harmonies of day's farewell,
In our hearts, the echoes swell.

Fading laughter lingers near,
Whispers soft, for us to hear.
Each moment, a fleeting spark,
As we drift into the dark.

With each fade, a new embrace,
Time will capture every trace.
In this symphony, we'll stay,
Bound by night, until the day.

Cascading Dreams of the Dusk

In the hour when shadows play,
Dreams begin to drift away.
Softly flowing like a stream,
Caught within the twilight's beam.

Whirl of visions, shadows blend,
Whispered secrets, time to tend.
Cascades of thought, they rise and fall,
Echoed softly, through it all.

As we glide on the gentle breeze,
Moments pass with graceful ease.
Hushed desires, whispered sighs,
Dance among the starry skies.

In this dusk, our hopes align,
Fleeting dreams are yours and mine.
As the night begins to weave,
Cascading thoughts, we dare believe.

Soft Murmurs from the Distant Edge

On horizons, echoes call,
Soft murmurs from the distant thrall.
Voices carried on the night,
Trimmed with shades of silver light.

With the stars, they weave a tale,
Of trust found beyond the veil.
Melodies from far-off lands,
Brush the heart with tender hands.

Through the quiet, truth resounds,
In the stillness, hope abounds.
Waves of longing gently swell,
In the whispers, we can dwell.

Listen close, the world speaks clear,
Soft murmurs, drawing near.
In the night, we find our place,
Through distant voices, we embrace.

Threads of Connection in Cosmic Stillness

In the quiet void where stars align,
Whispers of fate in shadows entwine.
Nebulas bloom with colors so bright,
Weaving our dreams in the fabric of night.

Across the dark sea of endless space,
We glimpse each other, a soft embrace.
Threads of connection, unseen yet strong,
Binding our hearts like an ancient song.

Galaxies spin in a timeless dance,
In every heartbeat, a cosmic chance.
Carried by light, our spirits take flight,
Threads of connection, igniting the night.

In this vast stillness, we find our truth,
The echoes of ages, the wisdom of youth.
In every silence, a story unfolds,
Threads of connection, the universe holds.

Luminous Footprints on Time's Shore

On the edge of the ocean where time stands still,
Footprints are fading, yet memories thrill.
Waves whisper secrets, they ebb and flow,
Traces of moments that come and go.

Sunrise paints gold on the waking tide,
Each luminous footprint, a journey to guide.
Echoes of laughter, the joy we share,
Carried by currents, the heart's quiet prayer.

In the twilight's glow, as shadows stretch long,
Footprints will vanish, but love stays strong.
In the sands of time, our paths intertwine,
Luminous footprints, forever they shine.

Treasures of yesterdays, sparkling like gems,
Stories remembered in the sea's diadems.
As night draws near, we embrace the shore,
Luminous footprints, forevermore.

Gazes Across the Distant Chasm

In the hush of twilight, our sights entwine,
Gazes across chasms, a bridge divine.
Hearts whisper secrets that words cannot tell,
In the stillness of dusk, where shadows dwell.

Through the mist of distance, your eyes find me,
A bond unbroken, like roots of a tree.
Stars glimmer softly, a celestial map,
Guiding us closer, bridging the gap.

In the depths of silence, our spirits align,
Gazes across the chasm, eternally bind.
In the tapestry woven of hope and despair,
We stand together, each moment laid bare.

Though miles may separate, our souls remain,
Gazes across the distance, love's sweet refrain.
In the heart of the night, we find our place,
Gazes across the chasm, a sacred space.

A Chorus of Fading Echoes

In the hollow of night where memories fade,
A chorus of echoes in shadows displayed.
Whispers of laughter, a gentle refrain,
Carried on winds like soft, falling rain.

Moments replay in the silence we share,
Each note a memory, laden with care.
As the stars listen, their glow softly weeps,
A chorus of echoes, in darkness it keeps.

As dawn breaks the silence, the echoes may wane,
Yet the heart holds fast to the joy and the pain.
In the tapestry woven, every thread glows,
A chorus of fading, yet love overflows.

In the rhythm of life, the past holds our hands,
Every echo a story that forever stands.
With each whispered moment, we gather and weave,
A chorus of echoes, in dreams we believe.

Untold Tales Beneath the Stars

In shadows deep where secrets lie,
Whispers of dreams kiss the night sky.
Constellations weave their silent song,
Each glimmering light a tale lifelong.

The moonlight dances on the sea,
Reflecting stories bold and free.
An owl calls softly from afar,
Guiding the lost beneath the star.

Forgotten paths of ancient lore,
Echo through twilight, evermore.
In fragile hearts, the echoes bloom,
As night unfolds, dispelling gloom.

Moments Wrapped in Evening's Warmth

Twilight drapes its gentle hand,
Caressing fields both green and bland.
A sigh escapes from trees so tall,
As evening whispers, night will fall.

In quiet corners, shadows blend,
Where laughter lingers, hearts commend.
The warmth of love embraces tight,
In moments wrapped, the world feels right.

Candles flicker in sacred space,
Soft glows reveal a cherished face.
Time pauses in this tender hour,
As souls unite and hearts empower.

Glistening Threads of Silent Waves

Upon the shore where silence reigns,
Gentle waves weave their soft refrains.
Each whispering crest a secret shared,
In twilight's glow, the ocean's bared.

Moonlit trails upon the blue,
Reflecting dreams in every hue.
Soft footsteps mark the sandy bed,
As stories rise like stars unsaid.

The tide retreats with tales of old,
In each ebbing glimpse, we behold.
The heart of the sea, a timeless dance,
In glistening threads, we find our chance.

Stirring the Stillness of Dusk

The sun descends with languid grace,
Painting the skies in an amber embrace.
Stillness reigns as shadows play,
A gentle pause before the day.

Birds hum softly their evening tune,
While crickets sing beneath the moon.
In every breath, a moment sighs,
As dusk unfolds its velvet skies.

Branches sway in a whisper's breath,
Carrying whispers of love and death.
In this still hour, we find our way,
Stirring the heart, come what may.

Nightfall's Sweet Embrace

The sun dips low, a fiery glow,
Shadows stretch long, as whispers flow.
Stars emerge in their silent grace,
Nightfall wraps the world in its embrace.

Crickets sing in the gentle breeze,
Moonlight dances through whispering trees.
Dreams take flight on the velvet air,
In night's sweet hold, we pause and stare.

Soft lullabies from the heavens call,
We find our peace in the night's thrall.
Lost in thoughts, we drift and roam,
Under the stars, we find our home.

The world is hushed, a tranquil sphere,
In this dark beauty, we draw near.
With every breath, the night unfolds,
A timeless tale, in silence told.

Distant Horizons in Dappled Light

Morning breaks on the tranquil sea,
Waves hum softly, wild and free.
Sunbeams dance on horizon's crest,
A canvas bright, nature's best.

Fields of gold greet the waking sun,
Life awakens, a day begun.
Gentle breezes weave through the trees,
Boundless vistas invite the ease.

Birds take flight in the warming air,
On distant paths, adventures dare.
With each glance, new wonders ignite,
Guided by hope, in dappled light.

Clouds drift slowly, a painter's brush,
In this calm world, we find our hush.
Embracing dreams on the rolling hills,
With every heartbeat, the soul fulfills.

Lurking Beneath the Fading Stars

In the quiet night, shadows creep,
Secrets hidden in silence deep.
Fading stars flicker, dimmed by time,
Whispers echo in the night's rhyme.

Among the trees, dark figures sway,
As if the night holds dark ballet.
Eyes glisten softly, in watchful gaze,
What lies beneath in the moon's haze?

Haunting echoes call from afar,
Memories linger like a distant scar.
In shadows cast, the truth may hide,
Lurking secrets, where fears abide.

Yet hope glimmers in fractured light,
A promise born in the heart of night.
With courage found beneath the veil,
We rise above, our spirits sail.

Journeys Through the Golden Hour

As daylight fades to an amber hue,
Paths unfolding, calling to you.
With each step, the world comes alive,
In the golden hour, we learn to thrive.

Laughter echoes through fields of gold,
Stories shared, as moments unfold.
The setting sun paints the sky aglow,
In its warmth, our spirits grow.

Time stretches wide, like an endless stream,
Adventures await in the tender dream.
With every heartbeat, we blaze a trail,
In the golden hour, we shall not fail.

Together we wander, through shadows and light,
Chasing horizons, hearts pure and bright.
In the beauty of dusk, we find our way,
Journeys crafted in the end of day.